Daily Readings from the Prayers of Samuel Johnson

edited by Elton Trueblood

Philosophy may infuse stubborness, but Religion only can give patience.
— Doctor Johnson

Templegate Publishers
Springfield, Illinois

ISBN 0-87243-159-2

Daily Readings from the Prayers of Samuel Johnson

Portrait of Samuel Johnson
by Sir Joshua Reynolds
(Haverford College Library)

Order of Prayers

HEALTH OF BODY AND MIND

FAMILY AND FRIENDS

BIRTHDAYS

NEW YEARS

WIFE'S DEATH

EASTER

Introduction

†

"Dr. Samuel Johnson's character—religious, moral, political, and literary—nay, his figure and manner, are, I believe, more generally known than those of almost any man," wrote Boswell in the Introduction to his *Journal of a Tour of the Hebrides*. In spite of this, however, Boswell considered it not superfluous to attempt to make a sketch of his famous subject. The attempt is still not superfluous, especially in regard to his religious convictions and the background of his religious writings.

Though all readers who know anything about Dr. Johnson know that he was a devout man, there are relatively few who know him as the author of genuine classics of Christian devotion. The average thoughtful reader is aware of Johnson's *Dictionary*, of his essays, especially the *Rambler*, of his studies in Shakespeare, of his poems, and of his *Lives of the Poets*, but there are few, indeed, who are equally acquainted with Johnson's prayers. Many, who know the few prayers used by Boswell in the *Life*, are not conscious even of the existence of almost a hundred more like them.

Dr. Johnson was a deeply religious man and a conscious upholder of Christian doctrine all his days. He was a steadfast, devout and affectionate member of the Church of England throughout his long life. Not only did he hold Christian principles with strong personal conviction, but he would not permit them to be flouted or treated lightly in his presence. That this was true is the unanimous testimony of both acquaintances and biographers. Boswell says, concerning Christian principles, that "he would not tamely suffer" them to be questioned and Mrs. Piozzi informs us that he paid no attention to the ordinary inhibitions of politeness when anyone depreciated religion or morality.

Johnson's conscious devotion to serious religious thought and practice began in 1729, at the age of twenty, and continued to his death at the age of seventy-five. Though his whole life was spent in the eighteenth century, and though he is sometimes regarded as the arch representative of eighteenth-century England, there is one important sense in which he was not at all representative of his age. The general mood of his age, among intellectuals, was one of open scoffing at the Christian faith. When Samuel Johnson was twenty-five years old, Joseph Butler could truly say, in the advertisement to the first edition of his *Analogy*,

> It is come, I know not how, to be taken for granted by many persons, that Christianity is not so much as a subject of inquiry; but that it is, now at length, discovered to be fictitious. And accordingly they treat it, as if, in the present age, this were an agreed point among all people of discernment; and nothing remained, but to set it up as a principal subject of mirth and ridicule, as it were

> by way of reprisals, for having so long interrupted the pleasures of the world.

Like his older contemporaries, Butler and Wesley, but in a way which differed from the ways of both of them as their ways differed from one another, Johnson set the whole power of his mind and character against infidelity. He went against the main current all his days and he never faltered. Having read William Law's *Serious Call*, while a student at Oxford, Johnson became convinced that it was possible to be a Christian with the consent of all his faculties. "I expected to find it a dull book (as such books generally are), and perhaps to laugh at it," said Johnson. "But I found Law quite an overmatch for me; and this was the first occasion of my thinking in earnest of religion after I became capable of rational inquiry." Johnson's conviction was strengthened rather than diminished with the passage of years. "From this time forward," says Boswell in a well-known passage, "religion was the predominant object of his thoughts."

Johnson's religious position was formed largely under the influence of men of strong intellect, among whom, in addition to Law, were Taylor, Pascal and Addison. Boswell tells us of the reading of the elegant prose of Jeremy Taylor and we know Johnson gave Boswell a copy of Pascal's *Pensées* on Good Friday, 1779. The two men took with them, on their journey through northern Scotland and the Hebrides, a contemporary book on prayer by Dr. Samuel Ogden who, according to Johnson, "fought infidels with their own weapons."

Though Johnson read many men on religion, he reserved his greatest praise for his predecessor in the use of the periodical essay, Joseph Addison. We have it on

Mrs. Piozzi's authority that Johnson once said, "Give nights and days, Sir, to the study of Addison, if you mean to be either a good writer, or what is more worth, an honest man." It is our author's admiration for Addison which gives us one of the best indications of his personal faith.

> As a teacher of wisdom, he may be confidently followed. His religion has nothing in it enthusiastic or superstitious: he appears neither weakly credulous nor wantonly skeptical; his morality is neither dangerously lax, nor impracticably rigid. All the enchantment of fancy, and all the cogency of argument are employed to recommend to the reader his real interest, the care of pleasing the author of his being.

Like Addison, Johnson deliberately sought to follow the Middle Way and thus proved himself representative of English mentality in general if not of the eighteenth century in particular. This love of the Middle Way is perfectly exemplified in one of his letters in which he says, "Let not the contempt of superstition precipitate you into infidelity, or the horror of infidelity ensnare you in superstition."

Johnson was far removed from religious fanaticism. He objected greatly to what he called "feelers," meaning thereby those who relied exclusively on religious emotion, and he objected likewise to any extreme practices. "Whoever loads life with unnecessary scruples, Sir, provokes the attention of others on his conduct, and incurs the censure of singularity without reaping the reward of superior virtue." He opposed the use of a special plain garb, saying, "A man who cannot get to heaven in a green coat will not find his way thither the sooner in a grey one." While Johnson was deeply religious he was not a religionist. "Religionist" he rightly understood as a term of abuse, defining the word in his *Dictionary* as "a bigot to any religious persuasion." This he sought not to be.

Though Johnson was no bigot, his religious conviction was so intense that it found its way into all aspects of his rich life. We find his faith in God expressed in the *Tour of the Hebrides*, in his *Letters*, his various groups of essays, in the memorabilia of his distinguished friends and in Boswell's *Life*, as well as in his specifically religious production, *Prayers and Meditations*. Though always a layman he wrote several sermons, one of them an undelivered funeral sermon on the occasion of his wife's death. His essays were written with the Christian faith always in mind, though it was often unmentioned. In the last paragraph of the last *Rambler* he said, reflectively, "The essays professedly serious, if I have been able to execute my own intentions, will be found exactly conformable to the precepts of Christianity and without any accommodation to the licentiousness and levity of the present age."

Johnson's religion was such that prayer came easily and naturally to his lips, almost without effort. It was normal to him. Describing his stroke of palsy to Mrs. Thrale, he wrote, "I was alarmed and prayed God that however he might afflict my body he would spare my understanding." How little his devotional practice represented an escape from the remainder of his life is shown by the fact that the prayer mentioned to Mrs. Thrale was composed in Latin verse, in order that he might try the integrity of his faculties. At another time he tried the integrity of his faculties by learning Dutch and reading

The Imitation of Christ in that language.

All that Johnson did in connection with religion was done seriously and reverently. He would not permit himself to engage in either prayer or Bible-reading in a half-hearted or loose manner. "The coldest and most languid readers of the word," said one of his contemporary biographers, "must have felt themselves animated by his manner of reading the holy scriptures." He was equally unwilling to condone irreverence in others.

Central to Johnson's religion was his fear of death and preoccupation with it. By his own argument this was no psychological oddity, but was a wholly reasonable position in view of the human predicament. The argument for the reasonableness of the fear of death was put succinctly in the *Rambler*, 110. "If he who considers himself as suspended over the abyss of eternal perdition only by the thread of life, which must soon part by its own weakness, and which the wing of every minute may divide, can cast his eyes round him without shuddering with horror, or panting with security; what can he judge of himself, but that he is not yet awakened to sufficient conviction?"

The stupid thing, Johnson thought, was to face death with easy optimism or with carelessness. He believed in God, he believed in an eternal moral order, he knew human life was finite, and he knew furthermore of his own failures and sins. He wrote to Mrs. Thrale on March 20, 1784, when he was very ill, a letter of moving sincerity and honesty, as follows:

> Write to me no more about dying with a grace; when you feel what I have felt in approaching eternity—in fear of soon hearing the sentence of which there is no revocation, you will know the

> folly: my wish is that you may know it sooner. The distance between the grave and the remotest point of human longevity is but a very little; and of that little no path is certain. You knew all this, and I thought I knew it too; but I know it now with a new conviction.

In spite of this deep gloom, Johnson went on to say, "I am now cheerful." And his cheer, like his gloom, came from his religious convictions. He was able to be cheerful in spite of a deep belief in divine judgment because he also had a deep belief in the gospel of salvation. But his ultimate faith never came easy. He had too keen a sense of human suffering for faith to have an easy victory in his life. He had a great hope shadowed by a great fear, and the fear was never far in the background.

Some readers of Johnson's prayers, noting his frequent request that he be saved from indolence and sloth, may suppose that this was some kind of affectation. There is abundant evidence that it was not. He did, of course, work hard at times, but, like most men, he had to drive himself to the labor of writing. Always he had a keen sense of the disparity between what he was able to accomplish and what was required. Always death was coming on apace, and time was running out. At the end of the highly moving essay, which is the *Idler* for February 10, 1759, he wrote, "The night cometh when no man can work." The quotation symbolizes the mood of urgency which informs so much of his interesting life.

A great part of Johnson's religious genius was the direct result of his keen sense of human misery. Of all blasphemies he rejected most vigorously the blasphemy of optimism. Thus he was saved from superficiality. He understood the Cross. The sense of human misery came on him especially when he was alone, late at night, and that is when most of his prayers were composed. Accordingly these productions are free from the easy faith which comes too quickly to its goal. His prayers are great, partly because they partake of the nature of tragedy.

Some writers have supposed that Johnson's rationality and Johnson's religious faith occupied two different worlds of thought which did not meet. Those who have not been able to combine satisfactorily their reason and their religion find it hard to believe that Johnson was able to do so. But we have his own testimony and that of his friends that he refused to divide his life into conveniently separated compartments.

That he had a powerful mind we cannot doubt. Moreover his mental power was by no means limited to the criticism and production of literature. An example of his intellectual versatility is shown in his original statement about infinity, a statement which is frequently echoed in advanced mathematical circles today. "Numeration," he said, "is certainly infinite, for eternity might be employed in adding unit to unit, but every number is in itself finite, as the possibility of doubling it easily proves: besides, stop at what point you will, you find yourself as far from infinitude as ever." Here is a common-sense observation consistent with the notion that mathematical infinity is merely a matter of syntax.

The best evidence of the application of Johnson's versatile mind to theology is his long review of *A Free Enquiry into the Nature and Origin of Evil*, by Soame Jenyns. Here are thirty-eight pages of careful reasoning, marked, as we might expect, by a rejection of all the easy answers. Much as Johnson despised the conclusions of Voltaire, he and the French thinker were in complete agreement in rejecting the fashionable philosophical optimism of the day. In short Johnson used his mind as vigorously in his religion as in anything else he cared about.

It is one of the merits of the recent biography of Johnson by Joseph Wood Krutch that Professor Krutch has stressed the great man's thoroughgoing rationalism. "He was too much of a rationalist not to welcome anything that would help make Christianity seem rational," writes Krutch. "But he was also too honest to accept specious arguments merely because they were on his side."

This last point requires amplification. Conscious as Johnson was of the difficulties in the way of Christian faith, difficulties so great that his faith, though strong, was never supine, he was always seeking extra corroboration. Especially he wanted some extra evidence of survival after death and he long hoped that this evidence might be forthcoming in ghostly appearances. But the will to believe was not enough. Though Johnson repeatedly investigated claims concerning communications with the souls of the dead, he maintained sadly that the evidence was not convincing. Of second sight he said, "I never could advance my curiosity to conviction, but came away at last only willing to believe." Here is the most striking proof of his intellectual honesty in matters of religion.

How strictly honest Johnson tried to be in his religious exercises is shown by the prayer of April 26, 1752, soon after the death of his wife. Believing strongly in the communion of saints, the scholar thought it wholly possible that the soul of his departed wife might continue to be an influence for good upon him, not merely by means of memory, but by direct contact. The prayer begins, "O Lord, Governour of heaven and earth, in whose hands are embodied and departed Spirits, if thou hast ordained the Souls of the Dead to minister to the Living, and appointed my departed Wife to have care of me, grant that I may enjoy the good effects of her attention and ministration, whether exercised by appearance, impulses, dreams or in any other manner agreeable to thy Government." The crucial word here is "if." Johnson hoped that his hypothetical proposition might be true, but he was too honest to affirm it without evidence.

So far was Johnson from avoiding any direct contact between his reason and his faith that he seriously considered, as he told Boswell on their tour of the Hebrides, writing a book in support of Christianity. Evidently he had something in mind similar to the book Pascal hoped to write, but never finished. As in the case of Pascal, however, we know something of what the primary argument in such a book would have been.

Johnson's strongest argument for the objective truth of Christianity was the series of events which the Bible records and which have a convincing quality that mere speculation never has. He was convinced, not by ideas, but by events. In addition he was greatly strengthened, as is reasonable, by the judgment of trustworthy and critical men. Recognizing how difficult it is to know the truth in great matters, he perceived that, in many areas, our chief help comes from the authority of disciplined insight. In historical research we are forced to rely on the testimony of those most qualified to know and least likely to be deluded. There is no other way. Likewise in religion, "testimony has great weight, and casts the balance." Johnson knew, in short, that the human equation, far from being wholly removable, is our ultimate court of appeal. "As to the Christian religion, Sir, besides the strong evidence which we have for it, there is a balance in its favour from the number of great men who have been convinced of its truth, after a serious consideration of the question."

Johnson's argument for immortality was wholly from the nature of justice as applied to the problem of evil. There is good reason to believe that God is and that He is just. But justice is never perfectly done in this life. Therefore, if God is not defeated, there must be another life in which the justice, denied here, is finally achieved. "Since the common events of the present life happen alike to the good and bad, it follows from the justice of the Supreme Being that there must be another state of existence in which a just retribution shall be made and every man shall be happy and miserable according to his works."

It was Johnson's intention to be an orthodox Christian at all points, avoiding all the extremes which lead to heresy and error. He believed in the objective efficacy of prayer; he believed in the Bible as genuine revelation; he believed in the reality of free will. "Sir, we know our will is free, and there's an end on it." In his *Dictionary* "Bible" was defined as follows: "The sacred volume in which are contained the revelations of God." There was, he believed, an objective moral order which we partly know, but which is as truly independent of our wishes as is an historical event or a natural law. In the *Adventurer*, 74, he speaks of "the everlasting and invariable principles of moral and religious truth, from which no change of external circumstances can justify any deviation." It was his purpose as a moralist to try to discover, by careful thought, what some of these principles are.

One result of Johnson's orthodoxy was his emphasis on external and formalized religious practices. His Christian doctrine, as well as his observation of human life, made him keenly aware of the fact that men need external reminders of their duty. Johnson was not caught by the specious reasoning of his day about the noble savage and about the beauty life might have if only the artificial structures of civilization were removed. He saw that life without the contrived supports of civilization is merely ugly and cruel.

In all this Johnson was helped by the Christian doctrine of original sin, which he deeply believed. Since man has a bias toward evil, so that even our most ideally constructed communities are tainted with the struggle for prestige and personal power, it is evident that men need the ministrations of the church. Even the best of men need continual reminders of their duty. They are bad enough with the external help which the church gives; how vile would they be without it! Johnson availed himself of the external aids of private and public worship, not merely for his own sake, but as a good influence on his fellow men. He made it a rule to attend more carefully when there was public prayer, but not a sermon, "as the people required more an example for the one than the other, it being much easier for them to hear a sermon."

The popular doctrine about the natural goodness of man Johnson saw as sheer romantic nonsense. "Mankind," he wrote, "are universally corrupt, but corrupt in different degrees; as they are universally ignorant, yet with greater or less irradiations of knowledge." So great is human corruption that we have no really good thing in human life unless it is artfully contrived. The way out, therefore, lies not in despising the help which the Bible and Church can give, but in using them as incentives. Man is such a creature that he dare not neglect any individual "incitement to do well." This is because we are men and not angels.

Johnson's concern for the externals of religion is shown in his respect for the day of rest, and for his religious employment of various important days of the year which served as reminders. The first of the three things he required of Sir Joshua Reynolds was that Reynolds would promise not to work on Sundays, and the second was that the painter would read a portion of Scripture each Sunday. He deplored the nonobservance of Good Friday. So great was Johnson's indolence that in spite of his theories and his advice he was not wholly regular in such practices himself. Though he was sure that Sunday observance was one of the chief buttresses of civilization, he made it clear that he opposed any tendency to keep the day with rigid severity and gloom. What he valued, as a support for the best in human life, was the rhythm of the week rather than dull monotony, and he prized the Sabbath because it provided for mankind this beneficent rhythm. "It should be different from another day," he told Boswell on their famous tour. The Sundays which he passed at home, according to Sir John Hawkins, were "spent in the private exercises of devotion, and sanctified by acts of charity of a singular kind: on that day he accepted of no invitation abroad, but gave a dinner to such of his poor friends as might else have gone without one."

In the last year of his life, Dr. Johnson had a serious conversation with Dr. Adams of Oxford on the subject of the production of a book of prayers. To the request that he compose some family prayers, Johnson replied, "I will not compose prayers for you, Sir, because you can do it for yourself." After this characteristic blast, the great man went on, "But I have thought of getting together all the books of prayers which I could, selecting those which should appear to me the best, pulling out some, inserting others, adding some prayers of my own, and prefixing a discourse on prayer." Not only did Johnson entertain such a plan, but he was actually offered, says Boswell, a large sum for a volume of devotional exercises. It is unfortunate that this, like many of Johnson's other plans, was never executed. But there is some satisfaction that so many of the actual prayers were saved from destruction when most of the intimate papers were destroyed. The collection now printed constitutes the closest approximation we can make to Johnson's intended volume on prayer.

Though the idea of producing a prayer book seems to have come late in Johnson's life, he had been writing devotional literature for many years. This literature consisted partly of prayers and partly of the author's comments on his own spiritual condition or resolutions to do better. He was inspired, more than most men, by recurring anniversaries, such as those of his own birth, his wife's death, the beginning of the year and Easter. The first prayer which he wrote was a birthday prayer in 1738. He was also moved to devotional writing by any new undertaking of a serious character, such as the *Rambler* in 1750, or the study of law in 1765. Just before he died, Johnson put all of this highly personal material together and, because he was too ill to edit it himself, handed the lot to the Rev. George Strahan, with permission to publish. Dr. Strahan undertook the laborious task of getting Johnson's unedited devotional manuscripts ready for publication and finally brought out a faithful reproduction of the material in 1785, under the title *Prayers and Devotions*. Because he feared that the authenticity of the work might be doubted, Dr. Strahan deposited the manuscripts in the library of Pembroke College, Oxford, where they remain. The present editor has had the privilege of using these manuscripts, which are well preserved. They appear on sheets of many shapes and sizes and show only the beginnings of classification.

That Dr. Strahan's decision was a difficult one is clear. Though many of the journal items were almost worthless and many of them highly repetitious, the editor of the posthumous work decided to publish everything and to arrange all, whether prayers or diaries, merely by reference to the time of writing. He was undoubtedly influenced in this course by the fact that, in the Pembroke manuscripts, some of the prayers are already imbedded in other matter. Though one can understand the basis of Dr. Strahan's decision, it remains true that this decision has not proved a wholly fortunate one.

The inclusion of all of the journal items along with the prayers, as is done in the *Collected Works*, and in Volume I of Birkbeck Hill's *Johnsonian Miscellanies*, is not fair to Johnson. Whereas the prayers are highly polished productions, the autobiographical fragments are not. Some of them are so intimate in reference that it is hard to believe Johnson expected them to be published. We must remember that he was an old and ill man when he handed the manuscripts to his friend. When we recall that some of the most unfavorable judgments of Dr. Johnson's character and religion, particularly those relating to his fear of death, have come from this source, it is not surprising that several of his closest friends were resentful that Dr. Strahan had allowed the work to appear. The inclusion of the journal items was more unfortunate still in the fact that it kept the prayers from appearing in their true glory. This is undoubtedly the chief reason why so many well-read people are surprised to learn that Johnson was the author of prayers at all.

The purpose of this volume is to allow the prayers to stand alone, with no encumbrances, so that they may become better known and consequently better loved. I have added captions to facilitate easy reference, but, wherever possible, these captions retain and employ Johnson's own phrases, as found in his appended notes.

In order to make the Prayers more useful and to keep closer to Johnson's own original purpose I have classified the Prayers according to eight major categories, and have added, at the end, the last of all Dr. Johnson's many writings, the prayer which he wrote just before he died, the manuscript of which is in the possession of Professor Chauncey B. Tinker of Yale University. The notation on the manuscripts leads one to believe that, had Johnson lived to edit his own work, he would have classified the prayers according to some such categories of human need as have been employed in the present volume. Within each major classification the chronological order has been preserved, wherever this is known.

Though the purpose of the present book is that of making Johnson's devotional classics available to modern readers, and is therefore not merely antiquarian, it has seemed best, nevertheless, to retain the peculiar punctuation and capitalization of the original manuscripts. These help to bring the reader closer to the eighteenth-century author. The fact that Johnson did not live to give these details the merit of consistency presents no serious problem to the modern reader.

The manuscripts of the prayers provide a remarkable revelation of important features of Dr. Johnson's character. Most of them show signs of much correction, both in thought and in style, the rejected phrases being, in some cases, so heavily blacked out that it is not possible to recover them. On the manuscript of the famous prayer on the *Rambler* the ejaculations "Lord help me" and "So be it" appear underneath the main text, but have been crossed out. Below the birthday prayer for September 18, 1758, Johnson wrote: "This year I hope to learn diligence."

Several of the prayers give the hour as well as the date of composition, most of them indicating hours in the middle of the night. The prayer for January 1, 1749/50 was composed "after three in the morning," while the birthday prayer for 1775, was written during "a sleepless night." Information about Johnson's general religious practices is provided by some of the manuscripts, as when the note appended to the Easter prayer for 1753 says: "This I repeated sometimes at Church."

Several of the prayers were evidently written more than once and sometimes the development of thought and style can be traced. Thus we find, on the back of the manuscript of the prayer for March 24, 1759, the following, which is apparently an earlier form of the prayer listed in the present collection under the caption "Change of Circumstances."

> O Lord, let the change which I am now making in outward things produce in me such a change of manners, as may fit me (for) the great change through which my wife has passed.

It is hard to overestimate the enormous influence on

Johnson of the death of his wife in March, 1752. This influence appears in many of his literary productions, but most vividly in his devotional writings. Whereas the numbers of the *Rambler* ended with Mrs. Johnson's death, the production of devotional writings was greatly accentuated by this sad occurrence. Of the one hundred Prayers printed in the present collection, only *five* were written before Mrs. Johnson died. All the Easter prayers were written after her death, the Doctor's meticulous care in the celebration of Easter throughout the remaining thirty-two years of his life being occasioned by his conviction that such care was in accordance with his deceased mate's wish.

Any sensitive reader is bound to be deeply moved by the way in which Johnson remembered his wife, turning his personal sorrow into a means of spiritual growth. In doing so he has given a worthy example to all who suffer bereavement and loneliness. The journal entry for Good Friday, March 28, 1777, says, "I remembered that it was my wife's dying day, and begged pardon for all our sins, and commended her: but resolved to mix little of my own sorrows or cares with the great solemnity."

How little the years dimmed his grief is shown by a journal entry five years later. "This is the day on which in 1752 dear Tetty died," he wrote. "We were married almost seventeen years, and have now been parted thirty." In view of the genuineness of his grief and the greatness of the man, there is reason to doubt the fairness of contemporary estimates of Mrs. Johnson which have long made the world think poorly of her. That she was not perfect the Doctor recognized. Even in one of the most moving of his prayers, that written four weeks after she died, he prayed not only that he might "imitate whatever was in her life acceptable," but also that he might "avoid all by which she offended." The bereaved man, we conclude, was aware in his wife's character of admirable traits unknown to those who did not love her.

It will generally be agreed that it is in those petitions penned by Johnson soon after his bereavement that he reached the greatest heights. It is hard to think of any prayer in our language which states so perfectly what a devout man may feel in sorrow as that written on May 6, 1752. It appears in this volume under the caption "After Thirty-nine Days." The petition "that neither praise may fill me with pride, nor censure with discontent" represents at its best Johnson's remarkable felicity of phrase.

The prayers as they now appear are *genuine classics of devotion.* This is shown both by their content and by their form. The form, for the most part, is that of the Collect, the form most demonstrated in the Book of Common Prayer. Trained from childhood in the use of this form, Johnson was conscious of standing in a noble tradition and added materially to it. The Collect form is a reasonably strict one, proceeding from Salutation to Ascription, to Petition, to Reason for Petition, to Conclusion. The whole is marked by a singular economy of phrase which permits neither padding nor digression. The Johnson prayers which show the most meticulous Collect style are the "Introductory Prayer," written March 25, 1756, and the Prayer on Volume II of the *Dictionary,* composed April 3, 1753. All the known prayers written by Johnson are included in this edition.

One of the most moving of the prayers in this volume was made at the bedside of his mother's maid, Kitty Chambers, as the serving woman lay dying. The journal entry for Sunday, October 18, 1767, is as follows:

> Yesterday, Oct. 17, at about ten in the morning I took my leave for ever of my dear old friend, Catherine Chambers, who came to live with my mother about 1724, and has been but little parted from us since. She buried my father, my brother, and my mother. She is now fifty-eight years old. I desired all to withdraw, then told her that we were to part forever, that as Christians, we should part with prayer; and that I would, if she was willing, say a short prayer beside her. She expressed great desire to hear me; and held up her poor hands, as she lay in bed, with great fervour, while I prayed kneeling by her, nearly in the following words: . . .
> I then kissed her. She told me that to part was the greatest pain she had ever felt, and that she hoped we should meet again in a better place. I expressed with swelled eyes, and great emotion of tenderness, the same hopes. We kissed, and parted. I humbly hope to meet again and part no more.

Here is one of the truly noble scenes of our history —the leading man of letters of his nation and century kneeling, in humble faith, by the bedside of his mother's servant. The worship of God broke down all distinctions of rank, no matter how important they might seem on other grounds. Johnson was made humble in the only way a man of his stubborn intellectual pride could be made humble, by an overwhelming sense of the reality of God which made him see his own life in its true light.

In the prayers printed on the pages of this book, the

reader may gain some insight into the character of a man who was marked above all by a rugged honesty which made him face repeatedly his own failures. Because such failure is a common human experience, uniting all men, even though they live in different centuries, and because the faith in God which is the ultimate reason for these prayers is independent of changing fashions, these noble words written in one century may speak to the condition of perplexed men and women living in the middle of another.

ELTON TRUEBLOOD

Dr. Johnson's Prayers

Amendment of Life

†

INTRODUCTORY PRAYER

O GOD who desirest not the death of a Sinner, look down with mercy upon me now daring to call upon thee. Let thy Holy Spirit so purify my affections, and exalt my desires that my prayer may be acceptable in thy sight, through Jesus Christ. *Amen*

NEGLECT OF DUTY

O LORD, in whose hands are life and death, by whose power I am sustained, and by whose mercy I am spared, look down upon me with pity. Forgive me, that I have this day neglected the duty which Thou hast assigned to it, and suffered the hours, of which I must give account, to pass away without any endeavour to accomplish thy will, or to promote my own salvation. Make me to remember, O God, that every day is thy gift, and ought to be used according to thy command. Grant me, therefore, so to repent of my negligence, that I may obtain mercy from Thee, and pass the time which Thou shalt yet allow me, in diligent performance of thy commands, through Jesus Christ. *Amen*.

IMPEDIMENTS

O GOD, heavenly Father, who desirest not the death of a Sinner, grant that I may turn from my Wickedness and live. Enable me to shake off all impediments of lawful action, and so to order my life, that increase of days may produce increase of grace, of tranquillity of thought, and vigour in duty. Grant that my resolves may be effectual to a holy life, and a happy death, for Jesus Christ's sake. *Amen*.

ENLARGEMENT OF CHARITY

ALMIGHTY and most merciful Father, who by thy son Jesus Christ hast redeemed man from Sin and Death, grant that the commemoration of his passion may quicken my repentance, encrease my hope, and strengthen my faith and enlarge my Charity; that I may lament and forsake my sins and for the time which thou shalt yet grant me, may avoid Idleness, and neglect of thy word and worship. Grant me strength to be diligent in the lawful employments which shall be set before me; Grant me purity of thoughts, words, and actions. Grant me to love and study thy word, and to frequent thy worship with pure affection. Deliver and preserve me from vain terrours, and grant that by the Grace of thy Holy Spirit I may so live that after this life is ended, I may be received to everlasting happiness for the sake of Jesus Christ our Lord. *Amen*.

REDEEMING THE TIME

O LORD, who wouldst that all men should be saved, and who knowest that without thy grace we can do nothing acceptable to thee, have mercy upon me. Enable me to break the chain of my sins, to reject sensuality in thought, and to overcome and suppress vain scruples; and to use such diligence in lawful employment as may enable me to support myself and do good to others. O Lord, forgive me the time lost in idleness; pardon the sins which I have committed, and grant that I may redeem the time misspent, and be reconciled to thee by true repentance, that I may live and die in peace, and be received to everlasting happiness. Take not from me, O Lord, thy Holy Spirit, but let me have support and comfort for Jesus Christ's sake. *Amen.*

A NEW LIFE

GRANT, I beseech Thee, merciful Lord, that the designs of a new and better life, which by thy Grace I have now formed, may not pass away without effect. Incite and enable me by thy Holy Spirit, to improve the time which Thou shalt grant me; to avoid all evil thoughts words and actions; and to do all the duties which thou shalt set before me. Hear my prayer, O Lord, for the Sake of Jesus Christ. *Amen.*

DILIGENCE AND PATIENCE

ALMIGHTY GOD, by whose mercy I am now permitted to commemorate my Redemption by our Lord Jesus Christ; grant that this awful remembrance may strengthen my Faith, enliven my Hope, and encrease my Charity; that I may trust in Thee with my whole heart, and do good according to my power. Grant me the help of thy Holy Spirit, that I may do thy will with diligence, and suffer it with humble patience: so that when Thou shalt call me to Judgement, I may obtain forgiveness and acceptance for the sake of Jesus Christ, our Lord and Saviour. *Amen.*

CORRUPT IMAGINATIONS

O LORD GOD, in whose hand are the wills and affections of men, kindle in my mind holy desires, and repress sinful and corrupt imaginations; enable me to love thy commandments, and to desire thy promises; let me, by thy protection and influence, so pass through things temporal, as finally not to lose the things eternal; and among the hopes and fears, the pleasures and sorrows, the dangers and deliverances, and all the changes of this life, let my heart be surely fixed, by the help of thy Holy Spirit, on the everlasting fruition of thy presence, where true joys are to be found. Grant, O Lord, these petitions. Forgive, O merciful Lord, whatever I have done contrary to thy laws. Give me such a sense of my wickedness as may produce true contrition and effectual repentance, so that when I shall be called into another state, I may be received among the sinners to whom sorrow and reformation have obtained pardon, for Jesus Christ's sake. *Amen*.

REPENTANCE

O MERCIFUL GOD, full of compassion, long-suffering, and of great pity, who sparest when we deserve punishment, and in thy wrath thinkest upon mercy; make me earnestly to repent, and heartily to be sorry for all my misdoings; make the remembrance so burdensome and painful, that I may flee to Thee with a troubled spirit and a contrite heart; and, O merciful Lord, visit, comfort, and relieve me; cast me not out from thy presence, and take not thy Holy Spirit from me, but excite in me true repentance; give me in this world knowledge of thy truth, and confidence in thy mercy, and in the world to come life everlasting, for the sake of our Lord and Saviour, thy Son Jesus Christ. *Amen*

ALMIGHTY and most merciful Father, whose clemency I now presume to implore, after a long life of carelessness and wickedness, have mercy upon me. I have committed many trespasses; I have neglected many duties. I have done what Thou hast forbidden, and left undone what Thou hast commanded. Forgive, merciful Lord, my sins, negligences, and ignorances, and enable me, by the Holy Spirit, to amend my life according to thy Holy Word, for Jesus Christ's sake. *Amen.*

Work and Study

†

BEFORE ANY NEW STUDY

ALMIGHTY GOD, in whose hands are all the powers of man; who givest understanding, and takest it away; who, as it seemeth good unto Thee, enlightenest the thoughts of the simple, and darkenest the meditations of the wise, be present with me in my studies and enquiries.

Grant, O Lord, that I may not lavish away the life which Thou hast given me on useless trifles, nor waste it in vain searches after things which Thou hast hidden from me.

Enable me, by thy Holy Spirit, so to shun sloth and negligence, that every day may discharge part of the task which Thou hast allotted me; and so further with thy help that labour which, without thy help, must be ineffectual, that I may obtain, in all my undertakings, such success as will most promote thy glory, and the salvation of my own soul, for the sake of Jesus Christ. *Amen*.

THE RAMBLER

ALMIGHTY GOD, the giver of all good things, without whose help all Labour is ineffectual, and without whose grace all wisdom is folly, grant, I beseech Thee, that in this my undertaking, thy Holy Spirit may not be withheld from me, but that I may promote thy glory, and the Salvation both of myself and others; grant this, O Lord, for the sake of Jesus Christ. *Amen*.

THE DICTIONARY

O GOD, who hast hitherto supported me, enable me to proceed in this labour, and in the whole task of my present state; that when I shall render up, at the last day, an account of the talent committed to me, I may receive pardon, for the sake of Jesus Christ. *Amen*

CHANGE OF CIRCUMSTANCES

ALMIGHTY GOD, heavenly Father, who hast graciously prolonged my life to this time, and by the change of outward things which I am now to make, callest me to a change of inward affections, and to a reformation of my thoughts words and practices. Vouchsafe merciful Lord that this call may not be vain. Forgive me whatever has been amiss in the state which I am now leaving, Idleness, and neglect of thy word and worship. Grant me the grace of thy Holy Spirit, that the course which I am now beginning may proceed according to thy laws, and end in the enjoyment of thy favour. Give me, O Lord, pardon and peace, that I may serve thee with humble confidence, and after this life enjoy thy presence in eternal Happiness.

And, O Lord, so far as it may be lawful for me, I commend to thy Fatherly goodness, My Father, my Brother, my Wife, my Mother. I beseech thee to look mercifully upon them, and grant them whatever may most promote their present and eternal joy.

O Lord, hear my prayers for Jesus Christ's sake to whom, with Thee and the Holy Ghost three persons and one God be all honour and glory world without end. *Amen*

THE STUDY OF PHILOSOPHY

O LORD, who hast ordained labour to be the lot of man, and seest the necessities of all thy creatures, bless my studies and endeavours; feed me with food convenient for me; and if it shall be thy good pleasure to intrust me with plenty, give me a compassionate heart, that I may be ready to relieve the wants of others; let neither poverty nor riches estrange my heart from Thee, but assist me with thy grace so to live as that I may die in thy favour, for the sake of Jesus Christ. *Amen.*

THE STUDY OF LAW

ALMIGHTY GOD, the Giver of Wisdom, without whose help resolutions are vain, without whose blessing study is ineffectual, enable me, if it be thy will, to attain such knowledge as may qualify me to direct the doubtful, and instruct the ignorant, to prevent wrongs, and terminate contentions; and grant that I may use that knowledge which I shall attain, to thy glory and my own salvation, for Jesus Christ's sake. *Amen.*

ENGAGING IN POLITICS

ALMIGHTY GOD, who art the Giver of all Wisdom enlighten my understanding with knowledge of right, and govern my will by thy laws, that no deceit may mislead me, nor temptation corrupt me, that I may always endeavour to do good, and to hinder evil. Amidst all the hopes and fears of this world, take not thy Holy Spirit from me, but grant that my thoughts may be fixed on thee, and that I may finally attain everlasting happiness, for Jesus Christ's sake. *Amen.*

ALMIGHTY and most merciful Father, who hast graciously supplied me with new conveniences for study, grant that I may use thy gifts to thy glory. Forgive me the time misspent, relieve my perplexities, strengthen my resolution, and enable me to do my duty with vigour and constancy; and when the fears and hopes, the pains and pleasures of this life shall have an end, receive me to everlasting happiness, for the sake of Jesus Christ our Lord. *Amen.*

THE STUDY OF TONGUES

ALMIGHTY GOD, giver of all knowledge, enable me so to pursue the study of tongues, that I may promote thy glory and my own salvation.

Bless my endeavours, as shall seem best unto Thee; and if it shall please Thee to grant me the attainment of my purpose, preserve me from sinful pride; take not thy Holy Spirit from me, but give me a pure heart and humble mind, through Jesus Christ. *Amen.*

THE STUDY OF GREEK AND ITALIAN

O GOD who hast ordained that whatever is to be desired, should be sought by labour, and who, by thy Blessing, bringest honest labour to good effect; look with mercy upon my studies and endeavours. Grant me, O Lord, to design only what is lawful and right, and afford me calmness of mind, and steadiness of purpose, that I may so do thy will in this short life, as to obtain happiness in the world to come, for the sake of Jesus Christ our Lord. *Amen.*

THE STUDY OF RELIGION

ALMIGHTY GOD, our heavenly Father, without whose help labour is useless, without whose light search is vain, invigorate my studies and direct my enquiries, that I may, by due diligence and right discernment establish myself and others in thy holy Faith. Take not, O Lord, thy Holy Spirit from me, let not evil thoughts have dominion in my mind. Let me not linger in ignorance, but enlighten and support me, for the sake of Jesus Christ our Lord. *Amen.*

THE LIMITS OF KNOWLEDGE

O LORD, my Maker and Protector, who hast graciously sent me into this world, to work out my salvation, enable me to drive from me all such unquiet and perplexing thoughts as may mislead or hinder me in the practice of those duties which thou hast required. When I behold the works of thy hands and consider the course of thy providence, give me Grace always to remember that thy thoughts are not my thoughts, nor thy ways my ways. And while it shall please Thee to continue me in this world where much is to be done and little to be known, teach me by thy Holy Spirit to withdraw my mind from unprofitable and dangerous enquiries, from difficulties vainly curious, and doubts impossible to be solved. Let me rejoice in the light which thou hast imparted, let me serve thee with active zeal, and humble confidence, and wait with patient expectation for the time in which the soul which Thou receivest, shall be satisfied with knowledge. Grant this, O Lord, for Jesus Christ's sake. *Amen*

Health of Body and Mind

†

RESTORATION OF SIGHT

ALMIGHTY GOD, who hast restored light to my eye, and enabled me to pursue again the studies which Thou has set before me; teach me, by the diminution of my sight to remember that whatever I possess is thy gift, and by its recovery, to hope for thy mercy; and, O Lord, take not thy Holy Spirit from me; but grant that I may use thy bounties according to thy will, through Jesus Christ our Lord. *Amen.*

BODILY ENJOYMENTS

O GOD, grant that I may practise such temperance in Meat, Drink, and Sleep, and all bodily enjoyments, as may fit me for the duties to which thou shalt call me, and by thy blessing procure me freedom of thought and quietness of mind, that I may so serve Thee in this short and frail life, that I may be received by Thee at my death to everlasting happiness. Take not O Lord thy Holy Spirit from me, deliver me not up to vain fears, but have mercy on me, for the sake of Jesus Christ our Lord. *Amen.*

TEMPERANCE

O LORD, without whose help all the purposes of man are vain, enable me to use such temperance as may heal my body, and strengthen my mind, and enable me to serve Thee. Grant this, O Lord, for the sake of Jesus Christ our Saviour. *Amen.*

DISEASES AND PERTURBATIONS

ALMIGHTY GOD, merciful Father, whose providence is over all thy works, look down with pity upon the diseases of my body, and the perturbations of my mind. Give thy Blessing, O Lord, to the means which I shall use for my relief, and restore ease to my body and quiet to my thoughts. Let not my remaining life be made useless by infirmities, neither let health, if thou shalt grant it, be employed by me in disobedience to thy laws; but give me such a sense of my pains, as may humble me before thee; and such remembrance of thy mercy as may produce honest industry, and holy confidence. And, O Lord, whether Thou ordainest my days to be past in ease or anguish, take not from me thy Holy Spirit; but grant that I may attain everlasting life, for the sake of Jesus Christ our Lord. *Amen.*

DELIVERANCE FROM DISEASES

GLORY be to Thee, O Lord God, for the deliverance which Thou hast granted me from diseases of mind and body. Grant, O gracious God, that I may employ the powers which thou vouchsafest me to thy Glory, and the Salvation of my soul, for the sake of Jesus Christ. *Amen.*

PATIENCE AND SUBMISSION

ALMIGHTY GOD, Creator and Governor of the World, who sendest sickness and restorest health, enable me to consider, with a just sense of thy mercy, the deliverance which Thou hast lately granted me, and assist by thy Blessing, as is best for me, the means which I shall use for the cure of the disease with which I am now afflicted. Encrease my patience, teach me submission to thy will, and so rule my thoughts and direct my actions, that I may be finally received to everlasting happiness through Jesus Christ our Lord. *Amen.*

RECOVERY

ALMIGHTY GOD, our Creatour and Preserver, from whom proceedeth all good, enable me to receive with humble acknowledgement of thy unbounded benignity, and with due consciousness of my own unworthiness, that recovery and continuance of health which thou hast granted me, and vouchsafe to accept the thanks which I now offer. Glory be to Thee, O Lord, for this and all thy mercies. Grant, I beseech Thee, that the health and life which thou shalt yet allow me, may conduce to my eternal happiness. Take not from me thy Holy Spirit, but so help and bless me, that when Thou shalt call me hence I may obtain pardon and salvation, for the sake of Jesus Christ our Lord. *Amen.*

OLD AGE

O GOD, most merciful Father who by many diseases hast admonished me of my approach to the end of life, and by this gracious addition to my days hast given me an opportunity of appearing once more in thy presence to commemorate the sacrifice by which thy son Jesus Christ has taken away the sins of the world, assist me in this commemoration by thy Holy Spirit that I may look back upon the sinfulness of my life past with pious sorrow, and efficacious Repentance, that my resolutions of amendment may be rightly formed and diligently exerted, that I may be freed from vain and useless scruples, and that I may serve thee with Faith, Hope, and Charity for the time which Thou shalt yet allow me, and finally be received to Everlasting Happiness for the sake of Jesus Christ, our Lord. *Amen*.

Family and Friends

†

HILL BOOTHBY

O LORD GOD, almighty disposer of all things, in whose hands are life and death, who givest comforts and takest them away, I return Thee thanks for the good example of Hill Boothby, whom Thou hast now taken away, and implore thy grace, that I may improve the opportunity of instruction which Thou hast afforded me, by the Knowledge of her life, and by the sense of her death; that I may consider the uncertainty of my present state, and apply myself earnestly to the duties which Thou hast set before me, that living in thy fear, I may die in thy favour, through Jesus Christ our Lord. *Amen.*

MOTHER

ALMIGHTY GOD, merciful Father, in whose hands are life and death, sanctify unto me the sorrow which I now feel. Forgive me whatever I have done unkindly to my Mother, and whatever I have omitted to do kindly. Make me to remember her good precepts, and good example, and to reform my life according to thy holy word, that I may lose no more opportunities of good; I am sorrowful, O Lord, let not my sorrow be without fruit. Let it be followed by holy resolutions, and lasting amendment, that when I shall die like my mother, I may be received to everlasting life.

I commend, O Lord, so far as it may be lawful, into thy hands, the soul of my departed Mother, beseeching Thee to grant her whatever is most beneficial to Her in her present state.

O Lord, grant me thy Holy Spirit and have mercy upon me for Jesus Christ's sake. *Amen*.

And, O Lord, grant unto me that am now about to return to the common comforts and business of the world, such moderation in all enjoyments, such diligence in honest labour, and such purity of mind that amidst the changes, miseries, or pleasures of life, I may keep my mind fixed upon thee, and improve every day in grace till I shall be received into thy kingdom of eternal happiness.

CATHERINE CHAMBERS

ALMIGHTY and most merciful Father, whose loving-kindness is over all thy works, behold, visit, and relieve this thy Servant, who is grieved with sickness. Grant that the sense of her weakness may add strength to her faith, and seriousness to her Repentance. And grant that by the help of thy Holy Spirit after the pains and labours of this short life, we may all obtain everlasting happiness through Jesus Christ our Lord, for whose sake hear our prayers. *Amen*. Our Father.

HENRY THRALE

ALMIGHTY GOD who art the Giver of all good enable me to remember with due thankfulness the comforts and advantages which I have enjoyed by the friendship of Henry Thrale, for whom, so far as is lawful, I humbly implore thy mercy in his present state. O Lord, since thou hast been pleased to call him from this world, look with mercy on those whom he has left, continue to succour me by such means as are best for me, and repay to his relations the kindness which I have received from him; protect them in this world from temptations and calamities and grant them happiness in the world to come, for Jesus Christ's sake. *Amen*.

LEAVING STREATHAM

ALMIGHTY GOD, Father of all mercy, help me by thy Grace that I may with humble and sincere thankfulness remember the comforts and conveniences which I have enjoyed at this place, and that I may resign them with holy submission, equally trusting in thy protection when Thou givest and when Thou takest away. Have mercy upon me, O Lord, have mercy upon me.

To thy fatherly protection, O Lord, I commend this family. Bless, guide, and defend them, that they may so pass through this world as finally to enjoy in thy presence everlasting happiness, for Jesus Christ's sake. *Amen*.

ILLNESS OF ANNA WILLIAMS

ALMIGHTY GOD, who in thy late visitation hast shewn mercy to me, and now sendest to my companion disease and decay, grant me grace so to employ the life which thou hast prolonged, and the faculties which thou hast preserved, and so to receive the admonition which the sickness of my friend, by thy appointment, gives me, that I may be constant in all holy duties, and be received at last to eternal happiness.

Permit, O Lord, thy unworthy creature to offer up this prayer for Anna Williams now languishing upon her bed, and about to recommend herself to thy infinite mercy. O God, who desirest not the death of a sinner, look down with mercy upon her; forgive her sins and strengthen her faith. Be merciful, O Father of Mercy, to her and to me: guide us by thy holy spirit through the remaining part of life; support us in the hour of death and pardon us in the day of judgement, for Jesus Christ's sake. *Amen*.

DEATH OF ANNA WILLIAMS

ALMIGHTY and most merciful Father, who art the Lord of life and death, who givest and who takest away, teach me to adore thy providence, whatever Thou shalt allot me; make me to remember, with due thankfulness, the comforts which I have received from my friendship with Anna Williams. Look upon her, O Lord, with mercy, and prepare me, by thy grace, to die with hope, and to pass by death to eternal happiness, through Jesus Christ our Lord. *Amen*.

DOCTOR TAYLOR

ALMIGHTY and most merciful Father, who afflictest not willingly the children of Men, and by whose holy will   now languishes in sickness and pain, make, I beseech (Thee,) this punishment effectual to those gracious purposes for which thou sendest it, let it, if I may presume to ask, end not in death, but in repentance, let him live to promote thy kingdom on earth by the useful example of a better life, but if thy will be to call him hence, let his thoughts be so purified by his sufferings, that he may be admitted to eternal Happiness. And, O Lord, by praying for him, let me be admonished to consider my own sins, and my own danger, to remember the shortness of life, and to use the time which thy mercy grants me to thy glory and my own salvation, for the sake of Jesus Christ our Lord. *Amen*.

Birthdays

†

1738

O GOD, the Creatour and Preserver of all Mankind, Father of all mercies, I thine unworthy servant do give Thee most humble thanks, for all thy goodness and loving-kindness to me. I bless Thee for my Creation, Preservation, and Redemption, for the knowledge of thy Son Jesus Christ, for the means of Grace and the Hope of Glory. In the days of Childhood and Youth, in the midst of weakness, blindness, and danger, Thou hast protected me; amidst Afflictions of Mind, Body, and Estate, Thou hast supported me; and amidst vanity and Wickedness Thou hast spared me. Grant, O merciful Father, that I may have a lively sense of thy mercies. Create in me a contrite Heart, that I may worthily lament my sins and acknowledge my wickedness, and obtain Remission and forgiveness, through the satisfaction of Jesus Christ. And, O Lord, enable me, by thy Grace, to redeem the time which I have spent in Sloth, Vanity, and wickedness; to make use of thy Gifts to the honour of thy Name; to lead a new life in thy Faith, Fear, and Love; and finally to obtain everlasting Life. Grant this, Almighty Lord, for the merits and through the mediation of our most holy and blessed Saviour Jesus Christ; to whom, with Thee and the Holy Ghost, Three Persons and one God, be all honour and Glory, World without end. *Amen.*

1757

ALMIGHTY and most merciful Father by whose providence my life has been prolonged, and who hast granted me now to begin another year of probation, vouchsafe me such assistance of thy Holy Spirit, that the continuance of my life may not add to the measure of my guilt, but that I may so repent of the days and years passed in neglect of the duties which thou hast set before me, in vain thoughts, in sloth, and in folly, that I may apply my heart to true wisdom, by diligence redeem the time lost, and by repentance obtain pardon, for the sake of Jesus Christ. *Amen*

1758

ALMIGHTY and most merciful Father, who yet sparest and yet supportest me, who supportest me in my weakness, and sparest me in my sins, and hast now granted to me to begin another year, enable me to improve the time which is yet before me, to thy glory and my own Salvation. Impress upon my Soul such repentance of the days misspent in idleness and folly, that I may henceforward diligently attend to the business of my station in this world, and to all the duties which thou hast commanded. Let thy Holy Spirit comfort and guide me that in my passage through the pains or pleasures of the present state, I may never be tempted to forgetfulness of Thee. Let my life be useful, and my death be happy; let me live according to thy laws, and die with just confidence in thy mercy for the sake of Jesus Christ our Lord. *Amen*.

1760

O ALMIGHTY GOD, merciful Father, who hast continued my life to another year grant that I may spend the time which thou shalt yet give me in such obedience to thy word and will that finally, I may obtain everlasting life. Grant that I may repent and forsake my sins before the miseries of age fall upon me, and that while my strength yet remains I may use it to thy glory and my own salvation, by the assistance of thy Holy Spirit, for Jesus Christ's sake. *Amen.*

1766

ALMIGHTY and most merciful Father, who hast granted me to prolong my life to another year, look down upon me with pity. Let not my manifold sins and negligences avert from me thy fatherly regard. Enlighten my mind that I may know my duty that I may perform it, strengthen my resolution. Let not another year be lost in vain deliberations; let me remember, that of the short life of man, a great part is already past, in sinfulness and sloth. Deliver me, gracious Lord, from the bondage of evil customs, and take not from me thy Holy Spirit; but enable me so to spend my remaining days, that, by performing thy will I may promote thy glory, and grant that after the troubles and disappointments of this mortal state I may obtain everlasting happiness for the sake of Jesus Christ our Lord. *Amen.*

1768

ALMIGHTY and most merciful Father, Creator and Preserver of mankind, look down with pity upon my troubles and maladies. Heal my body, strengthen my mind, compose my distraction, calm my inquietude, and relieve my terrours, that if it please thee, I may run the race that is set before me with peace patience constancy and confidence. Grant this O Lord, and take not from me thy Holy Spirit, but pardon and bless me for the sake of Jesus Christ our Lord.

1 7 6 9

ALMIGHTY and most merciful Father, I now appear in thy presence, laden with the sins, and accountable for the mercies of another year. Glory be to thee, O God, for the mitigation of my troubles, and for the hope of health both of mind and body which thou hast vouchsafed me. Most merciful Lord, if it seem good unto thee, compose my mind, and relieve my diseases; enable me to perform the duties of my station, and so to serve thee, as that, when my hour of departure from this painful life shall be delayed no longer, I may be received to everlasting happiness, for the sake of Jesus Christ our Lord. *Amen*.

1 7 7 1

ALMIGHTY and everlasting God, whose mercy is over all thy works, and who hast no pleasure in the Death of a Sinner, look with pity upon me, succour and preserve me; enable me to conquer evil habits, and surmount temptations. Give me Grace so to use the degree of health which Thou hast restored to my Mind and Body, that I may perform the task thou shalt yet appoint me. Look down, O gracious Lord upon my remaining part of Life; grant, if it please thee, that the days few or many which thou shalt yet allow me, may pass in reasonable confidence, and holy tranquility. Withhold not thy Holy Spirit from me, but strengthen all good purposes till they shall produce a life pleasing to Thee. And when thou shalt call me to another state, forgive me my sins, and receive me to Happiness, for the Sake of Jesus Christ our Lord. *Amen.*

1773

ALMIGHTY GOD, most merciful Father, look down upon me with pity; Thou hast protected me in childhood and youth, support me, Lord, in my declining years. Preserve me from the dangers of sinful presumption. Give me, if it be best for me, stability of purposes, and tranquility of mind. Let the year which I have now begun, be spent to thy glory, and to the furtherance of my salvation. Take not from me thy holy Spirit, but as Death approaches, prepare me to appear joyfully in thy presence for the sake of Jesus Christ our Lord. *Amen.*

1775

O GOD by whom all things were created and are sustained, who givest and takest away, in whose hands are life and death, accept my imperfect thanks for the length of days which thou hast vouchsafed to grant me, impress upon my mind such repentance of the time misspent in sinfulness and negligence, that I may obtain forgiveness of all my offenses, and so calm my mind and strengthen my resolutions that I may live the remaining part of my life in thy fear, and with thy favour. Take not thy Holy Spirit from me, but let me so love thy laws and so obey them, that I may finally be received to eternal happiness, through Jesus Christ our Lord. *Amen*

1777

ALMIGHTY and most merciful Father, who hast added another year to my life, and yet permittest me to call upon thee, Grant that the remaining days which thou shalt yet allow me may be past in thy fear and to thy glory, grant me good resolutions and steady perseverance. Relieve the diseases of my body and compose the disquiet of my mind. Let me at last repent and amend my life, and O Lord, take not from me thy Holy Spirit, but assist my amendment, and accept my repentance, for the sake of Jesus Christ. *Amen.*

1779

ALMIGHTY GOD, Creator of all things in whose hands are Life and death, glory be to thee for thy mercies, and for the prolongation of my Life to the common age of Man. Pardon me, O gracious God, all the offences which in the course of seventy years I have committed against thy holy Laws, and all negligences of those Duties which thou hast required. Look with pity upon me, take not from me thy Holy Spirit, but enable me to pass the days which thou shalt yet vouchsafe to grant me, in thy Fear and to thy Glory; and accept O Lord, the remains of a misspent life, that when Thou shalt call me to another state, I may be received to everlasting happiness for the sake of Jesus Christ our Lord. *Amen*

1780

ALMIGHTY GOD, my Creator and Preserver, who hast permitted me to begin another year, look with mercy upon my wretchedness and frailty. Rectify my thoughts, relieve my perplexities, strengthen my purposes, and reform my doings. Let encrease of years bring encrease of Faith, Hope, and Charity. Grant me diligence in whatever work thy Providence shall appoint me. Take not from me thy Holy Spirit but let me pass the remainder of the days which thou shalt yet allow me, in thy fear and to thy Glory; and when it shall be thy good pleasure to call me hence, grant me, O Lord, forgiveness of my sins, and receive me to everlasting happiness, for the Sake of Jesus Christ, our Lord. *Amen*.

1781

ALMIGHTY and most merciful Father, who hast brought me to the beginning of another year, grant me so to remember thy gifts, and so to acknowledge thy goodness, as that every year and day which thou shalt yet grant me, may be employed in the amendment of my life, and in the diligent discharge of such duties, as thy Providence shall allot me. Grant me, by thy Grace, to know and to do what Thou requirest. Give me good desires, and remove those impediments which may hinder them from effect. Forgive me my sins, negligences, and ignorances, and when at last thou shalt call me to another life, receive me to everlasting happiness, for the sake of Jesus Christ our Lord. *Amen*

1784

ALMIGHTY GOD, merciful Father, who art the giver of all good enable me to return Thee due thanks for the continuance of my life and for the great mercies of the last year, for relief from the diseases that afflicted me, and all the comforts and alleviations by which they were mitigated; and O my gracious God make me truly thankful for the call by which thou hast awakened my conscience, and summoned me to Repentance. Let not thy call, O Lord, be forgotten or thy summons neglected, but let the residue of my life, whatever it shall be, be passed in true contrition, and diligent obedience. Let me repent of the sins of my past years and so keep thy laws for the time to come, that when it shall be thy good pleasure to call me to another state, I may find mercy in thy sight. Let thy Holy Spirit support me in the hour of death, and O Lord grant me pardon in the day of Judgement, for the sake of Jesus Christ, our Lord. *Amen*

New Years

†

1744/5

ALMIGHTY and everlasting God, in whose hands are life and death, by whose will all things were created, and by whose providence they are sustained, I return thee thanks that Thou hast given me life, and that thou hast continued it to this time, that thou hast hitherto forborn to snatch me away in the midst of Sin and Folly, and hast permitted me still to enjoy the means of Grace, and vouchsafed to call me yet again to Repentance. Grant, O merciful Lord, that thy Call may not be vain, that my Life may not be continued to encrease my Guilt, and that thy gracious Forbearance may not harden my heart in wickedness. Let me remember, O my God, that as Days and Years pass over me, I approach nearer to the Grave, where there is no repentance, and grant, that by the assistance of thy Holy Spirit, I may so pass through this Life, that I may obtain Life everlasting, for the Sake of our Lord Jesus Christ. *Amen.*

1747/8

ALMIGHTY and most merciful Father, who hast not yet suffered me to fall into the Grave, grant that I may so remember my past Life, as to repent of the days and years which I have spent in forgetfulness of thy mercy, and neglect of my own Salvation, and so use the time which thou shalt yet allow me, as that I may become every day more diligent in the duties which in thy Providence shall be assigned me, and that when at last I shall be called to Judgement I may be received as a good and faithful servant into everlasting happiness, for the sake of Jesus Christ our Lord. *Amen*

1749/50

ALMIGHTY GOD, by whose will I was created, and by whose Providence I have been sustained, by whose mercy I have been called to the knowledge of my Redeemer, and by whose Grace whatever I have thought or acted acceptable to thee has been inspired and directed, grant, O Lord, that in reviewing my past life, I may recollect thy mercies to my preservation, in whatever state thou preparest for me, that in affliction I may remember how often I have been succoured, and in Prosperity may know and confess from whose hand the blessing is received. Let me, O Lord, so remember my sins, that I may abolish them by true repentance, and so improve the Year to which thou hast graciously extended my life, and all the years which thou shalt yet allow me, that I may hourly become purer in thy sight; so that I may live in thy fear, and die in thy favour, and find mercy at the last day, for the sake of Jesus Christ. *Amen*

1753, N.S.

ALMIGHTY GOD, who hast continued my life to this day, grant that, by the assistance of thy Holy Spirit, I may improve the time which thou shalt grant me, to my eternal salvation. Make me to remember, to thy glory, thy judgements and thy mercies. Make me so to consider the loss of my wife, whom thou hast taken from me, that it may dispose me, by thy grace, to lead the residue of my life in thy fear. Grant this, O Lord, for Jesus Christ's sake. *Amen.*

1 7 5 6

ALMIGHTY and everlasting God, in whom we live and move, and have our being, glory be to thee, for my recovery from sickness, and the continuance of my Life. Grant O my God that I may improve the year which I am now beginning, and all the days which thou shalt add to my life, by serious repentance and diligent obedience, that, by the help of thy holy Spirit I may use the means of Grace to my own salvation, and at last enjoy thy presence in eternal happiness, for Jesus Christ's sake. *Amen.*

1 7 5 7

ALMIGHTY GOD, who hast brought me to the beginning of another year, and by prolonging my life invitest to repentance, forgive me that I have misspent the time past, enable me from this instant to amend my life according to thy holy Word, grant me thy Holy Spirit, that I may so pass through things temporal as not finally to lose the things eternal. O God, hear my prayer for the sake of Jesus Christ. *Amen.*

1 7 6 6

ALMIGHTY and most merciful Father, I again appear in thy presence the wretched misspender of another year which thy mercy has allowed me. O Lord let me not sink into total depravity, look down upon me, and rescue me at last from the captivity of Sin. Impart to me good resolutions, and give me strength and perseverance to perform them. Take not from me thy Holy Spirit, but grant that I may redeem the time lost, and that by temperance and diligence, by sincere repentance and faithful Obedience I may finally obtain everlasting happiness, for the sake of Jesus Christ our Lord. *Amen*.

1767

ALMIGHTY and most merciful Father, in whose hand are life and death, as thou hast suffered me to see the beginning of another year, grant, I beseech thee, that another year may not be lost in Idleness, or squandered in unprofitable employment. Let not sin prevail on the remaining part of life, and take not from me thy Holy Spirit, but as every day brings me nearer to my end, let every day contribute to make my end holy and happy. Enable me O Lord, to use all enjoyments with due temperance, preserve me from unseasonable and immoderate sleep, and enable me to run with diligence the race that is set before me, that, after the troubles of this life, I may obtain everlasting happiness, through Jesus Christ our Lord. *Amen*

1769

ALMIGHTY and most merciful Father, who hast continued my life from year to year, grant that by longer life I may become less desirous of sinful pleasures, and more careful of eternal happiness. As age comes upon me let my mind be more withdrawn from vanity and folly, more enlightened with the knowledge of thy will, and more invigorated with resolution to obey it. O Lord, calm my thoughts, direct my desires, and fortify my purposes. If it shall please thee give quiet to my latter days, and so support me with thy grace that I may die in thy favour for the sake of Jesus Christ our Lord. *Amen*

1770

ALMIGHTY GOD by whose mercy I am permitted to behold the beginning of another year, succour with thy help and bless with thy favour, the creature whom Thou vouchsafest to preserve. Mitigate, if it shall seem best unto thee, the diseases of my body, and compose the disorders of my mind. Dispel my terrours; and grant that the time which thou shalt yet allow me, may not pass unprofitably away. Let not pleasure seduce me, Idleness lull me, or misery depress me. Let me perform to thy glory, and the good of my fellow creatures the work which thou shalt yet appoint me. And grant that as I draw nearer to my dissolution, I may, by the help of thy Holy Spirit feel my knowledge of Thee encreased, my hope exalted, and my Faith strengthened, that, when the hour which is coming shall come, I may pass by a holy death to everlasting happiness, for the sake of Jesus Christ our Lord. *Amen*.

1772

ALMIGHTY GOD, who hast permitted me to see the beginning of another year, enable me so to receive thy mercy, as that it may raise in me stronger desires of pleasing thee by purity of mind and holiness of Life. Strengthen me, O Lord, in good purposes, and reasonable meditations. Look with pity upon all my disorders of mind, and infirmities of body. Grant that the residue of my life may enjoy such degrees of health as may permit me to be useful, and that I may live to thy Glory; and O merciful Lord when it shall please thee to call me from the present state, enable me to die in confidence of thy mercy, and receive me to everlasting happiness, for the sake of Jesus Christ our Lord. *Amen*

1773

ALMIGHTY GOD, by whose mercy my life has been yet prolonged to another year, grant that thy mercy may not be vain. Let not my years be multiplied to encrease my guilt, but as age advances, let me become more pure in my thoughts, more regular in my desires, & more obedient to thy laws. Let not the cares of the world distract me, nor the evils of age overwhelm me. But continue and encrease thy lovingkindness towards me, and when thou shalt call me hence, receive me to everlasting happiness, for the sake of Jesus Christ, our Lord. *Amen.*

1774

ALMIGHTY GOD, merciful Father, who hatest nothing that thou hast made, but wouldest that all should be saved, have mercy upon me. As thou hast extended my Life, encrease my strength, direct my purposes, and confirm my resolution, that I may truly serve Thee, and perform the duties which Thou shall allot me.

Relieve, O gracious Lord, according to thy mercy the pains and distempers of my Body, and appease the tumults of my Mind. Let my Faith and Obedience encrease as my life advances, and let the approach of Death incite my desire to please Thee, and invigorate my diligence in good works, till at last, when Thou shalt call me to another state, I shall lie down in humble hope, supported by thy Holy Spirit, and be received to everlasting happiness, through Jesus Christ our Lord. *Amen.*

1776

ALMIGHTY GOD, merciful Father, who hast permitted me to see the beginning of another year, grant that the time which thou shalt yet afford me may be spent to thy glory, and the salvation of my own Soul. Strengthen all good resolutions. Take not from me thy Holy Spirit, but have mercy upon me, and shed thy Blessing both on my soul and body, for the sake of Jesus Christ our Lord. *Amen.*

1777

ALMIGHTY LORD, merciful Father vouchsafe to accept the thanks which I now presume to offer thee for the prolongation of my life. Grant, O Lord, that as my days are multiplied, my good resolutions may be strengthened, my power of resisting temptations encreased, and my struggles with snares and obstructions invigorated. Relieve the infirmities both of my mind and body. Grant me such strength as my duties may require and such diligence as may improve those opportunities of good that shall be offered me. Deliver me from the intrusion of evil thoughts. Grant me true repentance of my past life, and as I draw nearer and nearer to the grave, strengthen my Faith, enliven my Hope, extend my Charity, and purify my desires, and so help me by thy Holy Spirit that when it shall be thy pleasure to call me hence, I may be received to everlasting happiness, for the sake of thy Son Jesus Christ our Lord. *Amen.*

1779

ALMIGHTY GOD, merciful Father, who hast granted to me the beginning of another year, grant that I may employ thy gifts to thy glory, and my own salvation. Excite me to amend my life. Give me good resolutions, and enable me to perform them. As I approach the Grave let my Faith be invigorated, my Hope exalted, and my Charity enlarged. Take not from me thy Holy

Spirit, but in the course of my life protect me, in the hour of death sustain me, and finally receive me to everlasting happiness, for the sake of Jesus Christ. *Amen.*

1780

ALMIGHTY GOD, my Creator and Preserver by whose mercy my life has been continued to the beginning of another year, grant me with encrease of days, encrease of Holiness, that as I live longer, I may be better prepared to appear before thee, when thou shalt call me from my present state.

Make me, O Lord, truly thankful for the mercy which Thou hast vouchsafed to shew me through my whole life; make me thankful for the health which thou hast restored in the last year, and let the remains of my strength and life be employed to thy glory and my own salvation.

Take not, O Lord, Thy Holy Spirit from me; enable me to avoid or overcome all that may hinder my advancement in Godliness; let me be no longer idle, no longer sinful; but give me rectitude of thought and constancy of action, and bring me at last to everlasting happiness for the sake of Jesus Christ, our Lord and Saviour. *Amen.*

1781

ALMIGHTY GOD merciful Father, who hast granted me such continuance of Life, that I now see the beginning of another year, look with mercy upon me, as thou grantest encrease of years, grant encrease of Grace. Let me live to repent what I have done amiss, and by thy help so to regulate my future life, that I may obtain mercy when I appear before thee, through the merits of Jesus Christ. Enable me, O Lord, to do my duty with a quiet mind; and take not from me thy Holy Spirit, but protect and bless me, for the sake of Jesus Christ. *Amen.*

He that outlives a wife whom he has long loved, sees himself disjoined from the only mind that has the same hopes, and fears, and interest; from the only companion with whom he has shared much good or evil; and with whom he could set his mind at liberty to retrace the past, or anticipate the future. The continuity of being is lacerated; the settled course of sentiment and action is stopped; and life stands suspended and motionless, till it is driven by external causes into a new channel. But the time of suspense is dreadful."

— from a letter by Samuel Johnson

[illegible]

[illegible] man is likely to remain [illegible] the past or anticipate the future. The continuity of being is lacerated; the settled course of sentiment and action is stopped; and [illegible] motionless, till it is driven by external causes into a new channel. But the time of suspense is dreadful.

—from a letter by Samuel Johnson

Wife's Death

†

AFTER TWENTY-SEVEN DAYS

ALMIGHTY and most merciful Father, who lovest those whom Thou punishest, and turnest away thy anger from the penitent, look down with pity upon my sorrows, and grant that the affliction which it has pleased Thee to bring upon me, may awaken my conscience, enforce my resolutions of a better life and impress upon me such conviction of thy power and goodness, that I may place in Thee my only felicity, and endeavour to please Thee in all my thoughts, words, and actions. Grant, O Lord, that I may not languish in fruitless and unavailing sorrow, but that I may consider from whose hand all good and evil is received, and may remember that I am punished for my sins, and hope for comfort only by repentance. Grant, O merciful God, that by the assistance of thy Holy Spirit I may repent, and be comforted, obtain that peace which the world cannot give, pass the residue of my life in humble resignation and cheerful obedience; and when it shall please Thee to call me from this mortal state, resign myself into thy hands with faith and confidence, and finally obtain mercy and everlasting happiness, for the sake of Jesus Christ our Lord. *Amen.*

AFTER TWENTY-EIGHT DAYS

O LORD, our heavenly Father, almighty and most merciful God, in whose hands are life and death, who givest and takest away, castest down and raisest up, look with mercy on the affliction of thy unworthy servant, turn away thine anger from me, and speak peace to my troubled soul. Grant me the assistance and comfort of thy Holy Spirit, that I may remember with thankfulness the blessings so long enjoyed by me in the society of my departed wife; make me so to think on her precepts and example, that I may imitate whatever was in her life acceptable in thy sight, and avoid all by which she offended Thee. Forgive me, O merciful Lord, all my sins, and enable me to begin and perfect that reformation which I promised her, and to persevere in that resolution, which she implored Thee to continue, in the purposes which I recorded in thy sight, when she lay dead before me, in obedience to thy laws, and faith in thy word. And now, O Lord, release me from my sorrow, fill me with just hopes, true faith, and holy consolations, and enable me to do my duty in that state of life to which Thou hast been pleased to call me, without disturbance from fruitless grief, or tumultuous imaginations; that in all my thoughts, words, and actions, I may glorify thy Holy Name, and finally obtain, what I hope thou hast granted to thy departed servant, everlasting joy and felicity, through our Lord Jesus Christ. *Amen*.

AFTER TWENTY-NINE DAYS

O LORD, Governour of heaven and earth, in whose hands are embodied and departed Spirits, if thou hast ordained the Souls of the Dead to minister to the Living, and appointed my departed Wife to have care of me, grant that I may enjoy the good effects of her attention and ministrations, whether exercised by appearance, impulses, dreams or in any other manner agreeable to thy Government. Forgive my presumption, enlighten my ignorance, and however meaner agents are employed, grant me the blessed influences of thy holy Spirit, through Jesus Christ our Lord. *Amen.*

AFTER THIRTY-NINE DAYS

O LORD, our heavenly Father, without whom all purposes are frustrate, all efforts are vain, grant me the assistance of thy Holy Spirit, that I may not sorrow as one without hope, but may now return to the duties of my present state with humble confidence in thy protection, and so govern my thoughts and actions, that neither business may withdraw my mind from Thee, nor idleness lay me open to vain imaginations; that neither praise may fill me with pride, nor censure with discontent; but that in the changes of this life, I may fix my heart upon the reward which Thou hast promised to them that serve Thee, and that whatever things are true, whatever are pure, whatever are lovely, whatever are of good report, wherein there is virtue, wherein there is praise, I may think upon and do, and obtain mercy and everlasting happiness. Grant this, O Lord, for the sake of Jesus Christ. *Amen.*

AFTER TWO YEARS, MORNING

O GOD, who on this day wert pleased to take from me my dear Wife, sanctify to me my sorrows and reflections. Grant, that I may renew and practise the resolutions which I made when thy afflicting hand was upon me. Let the remembrance of thy judgements by which my wife is taken away awaken me to repentance, and the sense of thy mercy by which I am spared, strengthen my hope and confidence in Thee, that by the assistance and comfort of thy holy spirit I may so pass through things temporal, as finally to gain everlasting happiness, and to pass by a holy and happy death, into the joy which thou hast prepared for those that love thee. Grant this, O Lord, for the sake of Jesus Christ. *Amen*.

AFTER TWO YEARS, AT NIGHT

ALMIGHTY GOD, vouchsafe to sanctify unto me the reflections and resolutions of this day, let not my sorrow be unprofitable; let not my resolutions be vain. Grant that my grief may produce true repentance, so that I may live to please thee, and when the time shall come that I must die like her whom thou hast taken from me, grant me eternal happiness in thy presence, through Jesus Christ our Lord. *Amen*.

AFTER FOUR YEARS

ALMIGHTY GOD, our heavenly father whose judgments terminate in mercy, grant, I beseech Thee, that the remembrance of my Wife, whom Thou hast taken from me, may not load my soul with unprofitable sorrow, but may excite in me true repentance of my sins and negligences, and by the operation of thy Grace may produce in me a new life pleasing to thee. Grant that the loss of my Wife may teach me the true use of the Blessings which are yet left me, and that however bereft of worldly comforts, I may find peace and refuge in thy service through Jesus Christ our Lord. *Amen*.

AFTER SIX YEARS

ALMIGHTY and eternal God, who givest life and takest it away, grant that while thou shalt prolong my continuance on earth, I may live with a due sense of thy mercy and forbearance, and let the remembrance of her whom thy hand has separated from me, teach me to consider the shortness and uncertainty of life, and to use all diligence to obtain eternal happiness in thy presence. O God enable me to avoid sloth, and to attend heedfully and constantly to thy word and worship. Whatever was good in the example of my departed wife, teach me to follow; and whatever was amiss give me grace to shun, that my affliction may be sanctified, and that remembering how much every day brings me nearer to the grave, I may every day purify my mind, and amend my life, by the assistance of thy holy Spirit, till at last I shall be accepted by Thee, for Jesus Christ's sake. *Amen.*

AFTER TEN YEARS

O GOD, Giver and Preserver of all life, by whose power I was created, and by whose providence I am sustained, look down upon me (with) tenderness and mercy, grant that I may not have been created to be finally destroyed, that I may not be preserved to add wickedness to wickedness, but may so repent me of my sins, and so order my life to come, that when I shall be called hence like the wife whom Thou hast taken from me, I may die in peace and in thy favour, and be received into thine everlasting kingdom through the merits and mediation of Jesus Christ thine only Son our Lord and Saviour. *Amen.*

Easter

†

1753

O LORD, who givest the grace of Repentance, and hearest the prayers of the penitent, grant, that by true contrition, I may obtain forgiveness of all the sins committed, and of all duties neglected, in my union with the Wife whom thou hast taken from me, for the neglect of joint devotion, patient exhortation, and mild instruction. And, O Lord, who canst change evil to good, grant that the loss of my Wife may so mortify all inordinate affections in me, that I may henceforth please thee by holiness of Life.

And, O Lord, so far as it may be lawful for me, I commend to thy fatherly goodness the Soul of my departed wife; beseeching thee to grant her whatever is best in her present state, and finally to receive her to eternal happiness. All this I beg for Jesus Christ's sake, whose death I am now about to commemorate. To whom, etc. *Amen.*

1757

ALMIGHTY GOD, heavenly Father, who desirest not the death of a sinner, look down with mercy upon me depraved with vain imaginations, and entangled in long habits of sin. Grant me that grace without which I can neither will nor do what is acceptable to thee. Pardon my sins, remove the impediments that hinder my obedience. Enable me to shake off sloth, and to redeem the time misspent in idleness and sin by a diligent application of the days yet remaining to the duties which thy Providence shall allot me. O God, grant me thy Holy Spirit that I may repent and amend my life, grant me contrition, grant me resolution for the sake of Jesus Christ, to whose covenant I now implore admission, of the benefits of whose death I implore participation. For his sake have mercy on me, O God; for his sake, O God, pardon and receive me. *Amen*

1758

ALMIGHTY and most merciful Father, who hast created me to love and to serve thee, enable (me) so to partake of the sacrament in which the Death of Jesus Christ is commemorated that I may henceforward lead a new life in thy faith and fear. Thou who knowest my frailties and infirmities strengthen and support me. Grant me thy Holy Spirit, that after all my lapses I may now continue stedfast in obedience, that after long habits of negligence and sin, I may, at last, work out my salvation with diligence and constancy, purify my thoughts from pollutions, and fix my affections on things eternal. Much of my time past has been lost in sloth, let not what remains, O Lord, be given me in vain, but let me from this time lead a better life and serve thee with a quiet mind through Jesus Christ our Lord. *Amen*

1759

ALMIGHTY and most merciful Father, look down with pity upon my sins. I am a sinner, good Lord; but let not my sins burthen me for ever. Give me thy grace to break the chain of evil custom. Enable me to shake off idleness and sloth; to will and to do what thou hast commanded; grant me chaste in thoughts, words and actions; to love and frequent thy worship, to study and understand thy word; to be diligent in my calling, that I may support myself and relieve others.

Forgive me, O Lord, whatever my mother has suffered by my fault, whatever I have done amiss, and whatever duty I have neglected. Let me not sink into useless dejection; but so sanctify my affliction, O Lord, that I may be converted and healed; and that, by the help of thy holy spirit, I may obtain everlasting life through Jesus Christ our Lord.

And, O Lord, so far as it may be lawful, I commend unto thy fatherly goodness my father, brother, wife, and mother, beseeching thee to make them happy for Jesus Christ's sake. *Amen.*

1761

ALMIGHTY and most merciful Father look down upon my misery with pity, strengthen me that I may overcome all sinful habits, grant that I may with effectual faith commemorate the death of thy Son Jesus Christ, so that all corrupt desires may be extinguished, and all vain thoughts may be dispelled. Enlighten me with true knowledge, animate me with reasonable hope, comfort me with a just sense of thy love, and assist me to the performance of all holy purposes, that after the sins, errours, and miseries of this world, I may obtain everlasting happiness for Jesus Christ's sake. To whom, etc. *Amen.*

1764

ALMIGHTY and most merciful Father, who hast created and preserved me, have pity on my weakness and corruption. Deliver me from habitual wickedness and idleness, enable me to purify my thoughts, to use the faculties which Thou hast given me with honest diligence, and to regulate my life by thy holy word.

Grant me, O Lord, good purposes and steady resolution, that I may repent my sins, and amend my life. Deliver me from the distresses of vain terrour, and enable me by thy Grace to will and to do what may please thee, that when I shall be called away from this present state I may obtain everlasting happiness through Jesus Christ our Lord. *Amen.*

1765

ALMIGHTY and most merciful Father, who hatest nothing that thou hast made, nor desirest the Death of a Sinner, look down with mercy upon me, and grant that I may turn from my wickedness and live. Forgive the days and years which I have passed in folly, idleness, and sin. Fill me with such sorrow for the time misspent, that I may amend my life according to thy holy word; Strengthen me against habitual idleness, and enable me to direct my thoughts to the performance of every duty; that while I live I may serve thee in the state to which thou shalt call me, and at last by a holy and happy death be delivered from the struggles and sorrows of this life, and obtain eternal happiness by thy mercy, for the sake of Jesus Christ our Lord. *Amen.*

1766

ALMIGHTY and most merciful Father! before whom I now appear laden with the sins of another year, suffer me yet again to call upon Thee for pardon and peace.

O God! grant me repentance, grant me reformation. Grant that I may be no longer distracted with doubts, and harassed with vain terrors. Grant that I may no longer linger in perplexity, nor waste in idleness that life which Thou hast given and preserved. Grant that I may serve Thee in firm faith and diligent endeavour, and that I may discharge the duties of my calling with tranquility and constancy. Take not, O God, Thy holy Spirit from me; but grant that I may so direct my life by Thy holy laws, as that, when Thou shalt call me hence, I may pass by a holy and happy death to a life of everlasting and unchangeable joy, for the sake of Jesus Christ our Lord. *Amen.*

1770

ALMIGHTY and everlasting God, who hast preserved me by thy fatherly care through all the years of my past Life, and now permittest me again to commemorate the sufferings and the merits of our Lord and Saviour Jesus Christ grant me so to partake of this holy Rite, that the disquiet of my mind may be appeased, that my Faith may be encreased, my hope strengthened, and my Life regulated by thy Will. Make me truly thankful for that portion of health which thy mercy has restored, and enable me to use the remains of Life to thy glory and my own salvation. Take not from me O Lord thy Holy Spirit. Extinguish in my mind all sinful and inordinate desires. Let me resolve to do that which is right, and let me by thy help keep my resolutions. Let me, if it be best for me, at last know peace and comfort, but whatever state of life Thou shalt appoint me let me end it by a happy death, and enjoy eternal happiness in thy presence, for the sake of Jesus Christ our Lord. *Amen.*

1771

ALMIGHTY and most merciful Father, I am now about to commemorate once more in thy presence, the redemption of the world by our Lord and Saviour thy Son Jesus Christ. Grant, O most merciful God, that the benefit of his sufferings may be extended to me. Grant me Faith, grant me repentance. Illuminate me with thy Holy Spirit. Enable me to form good purposes, and to bring these purposes to good effect. Let me so dispose my time, that I may discharge the duties to which thou shalt vouchsafe to call me, and let that degree of health, to which thy mercy has restored me be employed to thy Glory. O God invigorate my understanding, compose my perturbations, recall my wanderings, and calm my thoughts, that having lived while thou shalt grant me life, to do good and to praise Thee, I may when thy call shall summon me to another state, receive mercy from thee, for Jesus Christ's sake. *Amen.*

1772

ALMIGHTY GOD, merciful Father, who hatest nothing that thou hast made, look down with pity on my sinfulness and weakness. Strengthen, O Lord, my mind, deliver me from needless terrours. Enable me to correct all inordinate desires, to eject all evil thoughts, to reform all sinful habits, and so to amend my life, that when at the end of my days thou shalt call me hence, I may depart in peace, and be received into everlasting happiness, for the sake of Jesus Christ our Lord. *Amen.*

1773

ALMIGHTY GOD, by whose mercy I am now about to commemorate the death of my Redeemer, grant that from this time I may so live as that his death may be efficacious to my eternal happiness. Enable me to conquer all evil customs. Deliver me from evil and vexatious thoughts. Grant me light to discover my duty, and Grace to perform it. As my life advances, let me become more pure, and more holy. Take not from me thy Holy Spirit, but grant that I may serve thee with diligence and confidence; and when thou shalt call me hence, receive me to everlasting happiness, for the sake of Jesus Christ our Lord. *Amen.*

1775

ALMIGHTY GOD, heavenly Father, whose mercy is over all thy works, look with pity on my miseries and sins. Suffer me to commemorate in thy presence my redemption by thy Son Jesus Christ. Enable me so to repent of my misspent time that I may pass the residue of my life in thy fear and to thy glory. Relieve, O Lord, as seemeth best unto thee, the infirmities of my body, and the perturbations of my mind. Fill my thoughts with awful love of thy Goodness, with just fear of thine Anger, and with humble confidence in thy Mercy. Let me study thy laws, and labour in the duties which thou shalt set before me. Take not from me thy Holy Spirit, but incite in me such good desires as may produce diligent endeavours after thy Glory and my own salvation; and when, after hopes and fears, and joys and sorrows thou shalt call me hence, receive me to eternal happiness, for the Sake of Jesus Christ our Lord. *Amen.*

1776

ALMIGHTY and most merciful Father, who hast preserved me by thy tender forbearance, once more to commemorate thy Love in the Redemption of the world, grant that I may so live the residue of my days, as to obtain thy mercy when thou shalt call me from the present state. Illuminate my thoughts with knowledge, and inflame my heart with holy desires. Grant me to resolve well, and keep my resolutions. Take not from me thy Holy Spirit, but in life and in death have mercy on me for Jesus Christ's sake. *Amen.*

1777

ALMIGHTY and most merciful Father, who seest all our miseries, and knowest all our necessities, Look down upon me, and pity me. Defend me from the violent incursions of evil thoughts, and enable me to form and keep such resolutions as may conduce to the discharge of the duties which thy Providence shall appoint me, and so help me by thy Holy Spirit, that my heart may surely there be fixed where true joys are to be found, and that I may serve Thee with pure affection and a cheerful mind.

Have mercy upon me, O God, have mercy upon me; years and infirmities oppress me, terrour and anxiety beset me. Have mercy upon me, my Creatour and my Judge. In all dangers protect me, in all perplexities relieve and free me, and so help me by thy Holy Spirit, that I may now so commemorate the death of thy Son our Saviour Jesus Christ as that when this short and painful life shall have an end, I may for his sake be received to everlasting happiness. *Amen.*

1778

ALMIGHTY and most merciful Father, suffer me once more to commemorate the death of thy Son Jesus Christ, my Saviour and Redeemer, and make the memorial of his death profitable to my salvation, by strengthening my Faith in his merits, and quickening my obedience to his laws. Remove from me, O God, all inordinate desires, all corrupt passions, & all vain terrours; and fill me with zeal for thy glory, and with confidence in thy mercy. Make me to love all men, and enable me to use thy gifts, whatever thou shalt bestow, to the benefit of my fellow creatures. So lighten the weight of years, and so mitigate the afflictions of disease that I may continue fit for thy service, and useful in my station. And so let me pass through this life by the guidance of thy Holy Spirit, that at last I may enter into eternal joy, through Jesus Christ our Lord. *Amen.*

1779

ALMIGHTY GOD, by thy merciful continuance of my life, I come once more to commemorate the sufferings and death of thy Son Jesus Christ, and to implore that mercy which for his sake thou shewest to sinners. Forgive me my sins, O Lord, and enable me to forsake them. Ease, if it shall please thee, the anxieties of my mind, and relieve the infirmities of my Body. Let me not be disturbed by unnecessary terrours, and let not the weakness of age make me unable to amend my life. O Lord, take not from me thy Holy Spirit, but receive my petitions, succour and comfort me, and let me so pass the remainder of my days, that when thou shalt call me hence I may enter into eternal happiness through Jesus Christ our Lord. *Amen.*

1781

ALMIGHTY GOD, merciful Father, by whose Protection I have been preserved, and by whose clemency I have been spared, grant that the life which thou hast so long continued may be no longer wasted in idleness or corrupted by wickedness. Let my future purposes be good, and let not my good purposes be vain. Free me O Lord from vain terrours, and strengthen me in diligent obedience to thy laws. Take not from me thy Holy Spirit, but enable me so to commemorate the death of my Saviour Jesus Christ, that I may be made partaker of his merits, and may finally, for his sake obtain everlasting happiness. *Amen*.

1784

ALMIGHTY GOD, my Creator and my Judge, who givest life and takest it away, enable me to return sincere and humble thanks for my late deliverance from imminent death. So govern my future life by thy Holy Spirit, that every day which thou shalt permit to pass over me, may be spent in thy service, and leave me less tainted with wickedness, and more submissive to thy will.

Enable me, O Lord, to glorify thee for that knowledge of my Corruption, and that sense of thy wrath, which my disease and weakness, and danger awakened in my mind. Give me such sorrow as may purify my heart, such indignation as may quench all confidence in myself, and such repentance as may by the intercession of my Redeemer obtain pardon. Let the commemoration of the sufferings and Death of thy Son which I am now, by thy favour, once more permitted to make, fill me with faith, hope, and charity. Let my purposes be good and my resolutions unshaken, and let me not be hindred or distracted by vain and useless fears, but through the time which yet remains guide me by thy Holy Spirit, and finally receive me to everlasting life, for the sake of Jesus Christ our Lord and Saviour. *Amen*.

Last Prayer

†

ALMIGHTY and most merciful Father, I am now, as to human eyes it seems, about to commemorate, for the last time, the death of thy Son Jesus Christ our Saviour and Redeemer. Grant, O Lord, that my whole hope and confidence may be in his merits, and his mercy; enforce and accept my imperfect repentance; make this commemoration available to the confirmation of my faith, the establishment of my hope, and the enlargement of my charity; and make the death of thy Son Jesus Christ effectual to my redemption. Have mercy upon me, and pardon the multitude of my offences. Bless my friends; have mercy upon all men. Support me, by the grace of thy Holy Spirit, in the days of weakness, and at the hour of death; and receive me, at my death, to everlasting happiness, for the sake of Jesus Christ. *Amen*.

The Daily Readings Series
General Editor: Robert Llewelyn

Daily Readings with Julian of Norwich, Vol. 1
Robert Llewelyn

Daily Readings with Julian of Norwich, Vol. 2
Robert Llewelyn

Daily Readings from 'The Cloud of Unknowing'
Robert Llewelyn

Daily Readings with Brother Lawrence
Robert Llewelyn

Daily Readings with Jean-Pierre de Caussade
Robert Llewelyn

Daily Readings with St John of the Cross
Sister Elizabeth Ruth ODC

Daily Readings with St Teresa of Avila
Sister Mary ODC

Daily Readings with St Francis de Sales
Michael Hollings

Daily Readings from Prayers & Praises in the Celtic Tradition
A.M. Allchin and Esther de Waal

Daily Readings with St Augustine
Dame Maura Sée OSB

Daily Readings with William Law
Robert Llewelyn and Edward Moss

Daily Readings with St Thérèse of Lisieux
Michael Hollings

Daily Readings with John Wesley
Arthur Skevington Wood

Daily Readings with Martin Luther
James Atkinson

Daily Readings from the Prayers of Samuel Johnson
Elton Trueblood

Daily Readings from Quaker Spirituality
Edward Cell